Library of Congress Cataloging-in-Publication Data

Back, Christine.
    Tadpole and frog.

    (Stopwatch books)
    Includes index.
    Summary: Photographs follow the development of a
frog from egg to tadpole to frog.
    I. Frogs—Development—Juvenile literature.
2. Tadpoles—Development—Juvenile literature.
3. Amphibians—Development—Juvenile literature.
[I. Frogs—Development. 2. Tadpoles—Development.
3. Metamorphosis] I. Watts, Barrie, ill. II. Title.
III. Series.
QL668.E2B27 1986   597.8043   86-10049
ISBN 0-382-09293-7
ISBN 0-382-09285-6 (lib. bdg.)

First published by A & C Black (Publishers) Limited
35 Bedford Row, London WC1R 4JH

© 1984 A&C Black (Publishers) Limited

Published in the United States in 1986
by Silver Burdett Company
Englewood Cliffs, New Jersey

Acknowledgements
The artwork is by B L Kearley Ltd.

Tadpole and frog

Christine Back
Photographs by Barrie Watts

Stopwatch books

Silver Burdett Press • Englewood Cliffs, New Jersey

Here is some frog spawn.

Have you ever looked at a pond or a ditch and found some frog spawn?

You can see some frog spawn in the photograph. Look at the black dots in the frog spawn. The dots are frog eggs. Some of these eggs will turn into young frogs, like this one.

This book tells you how the eggs turn into young frogs.

Here are a male frog and a female frog.
The female frog is laying her eggs.

In spring, frogs lay their eggs in ponds and ditches.
Look at the photograph. The male frog is on top of the
female frog. He is waiting for her to lay some eggs.

The female frog lays hundreds of eggs in the water.
The male frog covers the eggs with liquid from his body.

The eggs sink to the bottom of the pond. Then the frogs
swim away. They do not stay to look after their eggs.

Each egg is inside a ball of jelly.

Here is an egg inside its jelly ball.

In this photograph the jelly ball is shown very large.
In real life, it is about as big as a pea.

The jelly balls stick together. We call them frog spawn.
They float to the top of the pond. The water is warmer
at the top of the pond. This helps the eggs to grow.
Soon the eggs start to change shape. The outside of
each egg begins to look bumpy.

The eggs change into tadpoles.

The eggs change shape very quickly.
After four days, they look like this.

After seven days, the eggs have almost turned into
tadpoles. Look at the big photograph. Can you see the
tadpole's head and tail?

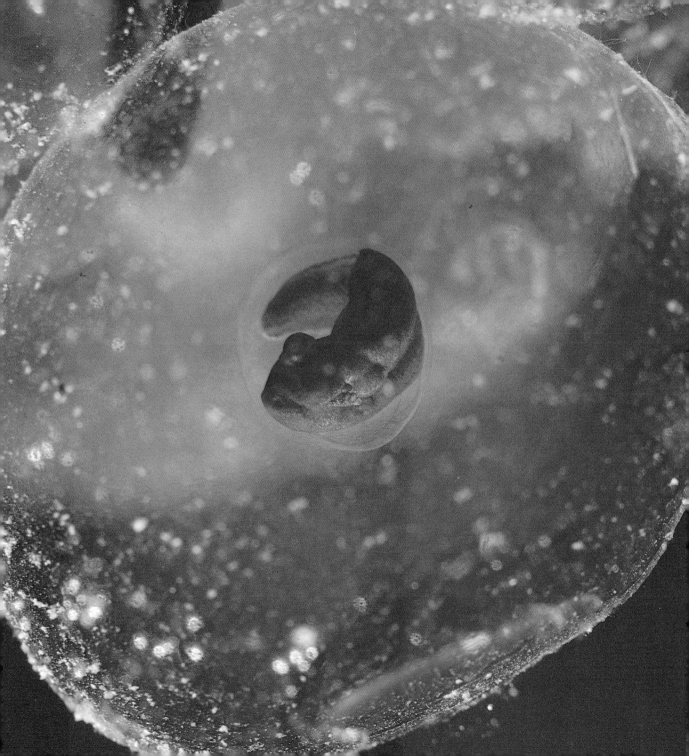

The tadpoles come out of the jelly balls.

After ten days, the tadpoles are ready to come out of the jelly balls. The jelly gets softer and the tadpoles wriggle out, like this.

Look at the big photograph. The tadpoles stay together. They rest near the jelly, or on plants.

The tadpoles can breathe underwater.

Each tadpole breathes through feathery gills
on the outside of its body. Look at the photograph.
Can you see the tadpole's gills?

Here is a drawing of a tadpole with gills.

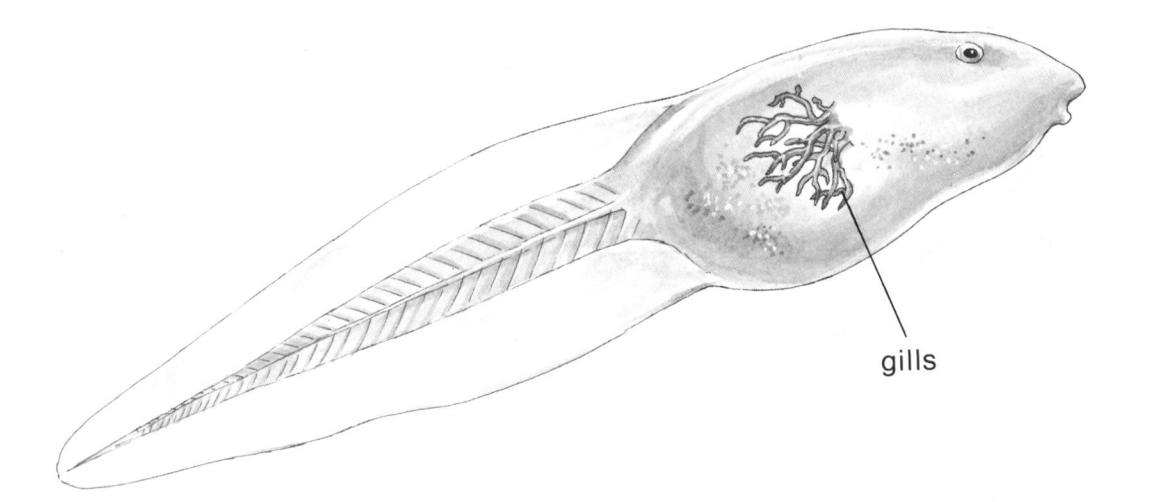

gills

The tadpole swims by wiggling its tail. It eats tiny
plants that grow in the water.

The tadpole grows back legs.

After five weeks, the tadpole has grown back legs. Its outside gills have disappeared. The tadpole can still breathe underwater. Now it breathes through gills which are inside its body.

The tiny tadpoles have many enemies.

This tadpole is being attacked by a water scorpion. Many tadpoles are eaten by other animals.

Now the tadpole cannot breathe underwater.

After about six weeks, the tadpole stops using its gills.
The tadpole grows lungs and breathes air like we do.
This means that the tadpole has to come to the top of
the water to breathe.

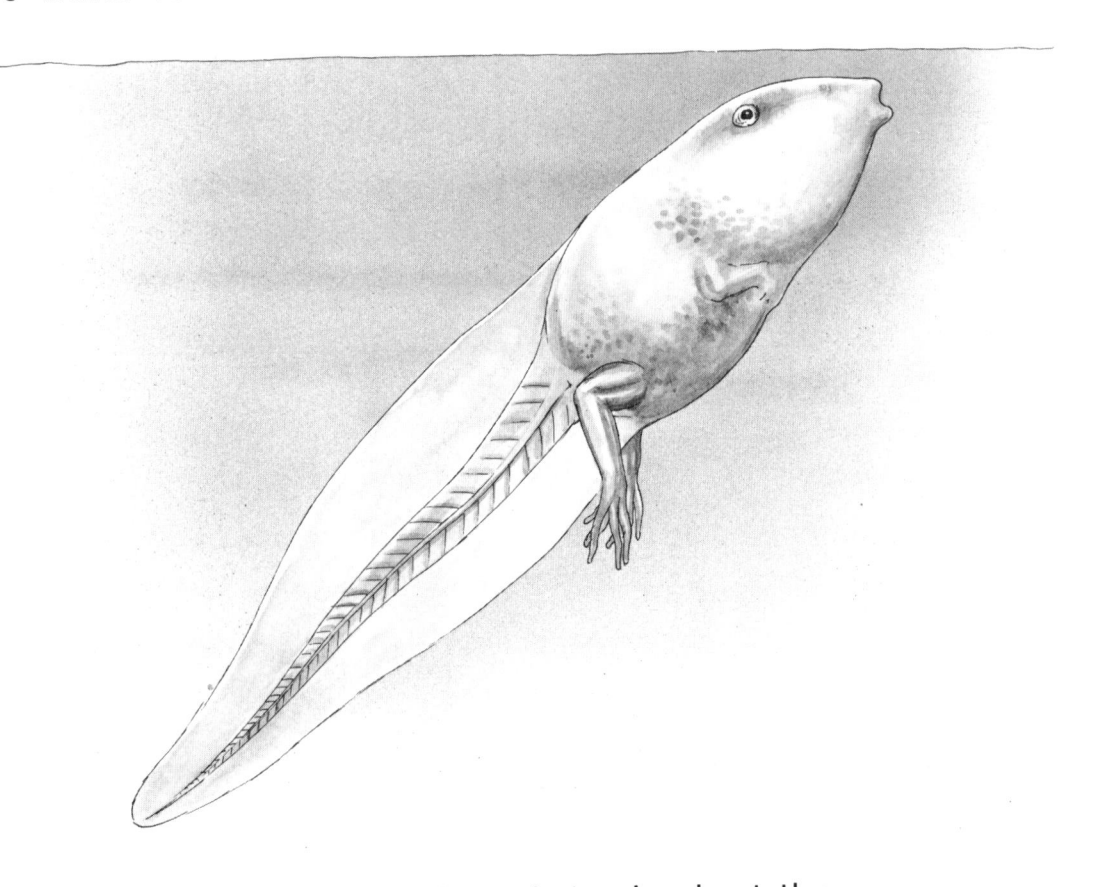

Soon the tadpole grows front legs. Look at the
photograph. This tadpole is ten weeks old.

The tadpole eats small animals.

The tadpole starts to eat small animals
that live in the water.

Look at the drawing.

Can you see that the tadpole's tail is getting shorter?
Soon the tadpole begins to look more like a frog.
Look at the photograph. This tadpole is twelve weeks old.

The tadpole has turned into a frog.
It lives on land.

After fifteen weeks, the tadpole has turned into
a tiny frog.

The frog leaves the water and lives on land.
It uses its strong back legs to jump from place to place.
But the frog still goes back to the pond for a swim.

The tiny frog grows up.

Soon the frog moves away from the pond. The frog lives in damp places and it eats insects, beetles, and worms.

The frog slowly grows up to look like its mother or father. Look at the photograph. This female frog is a year old. Next spring, the frog will go to a pond and lay some eggs, like these.

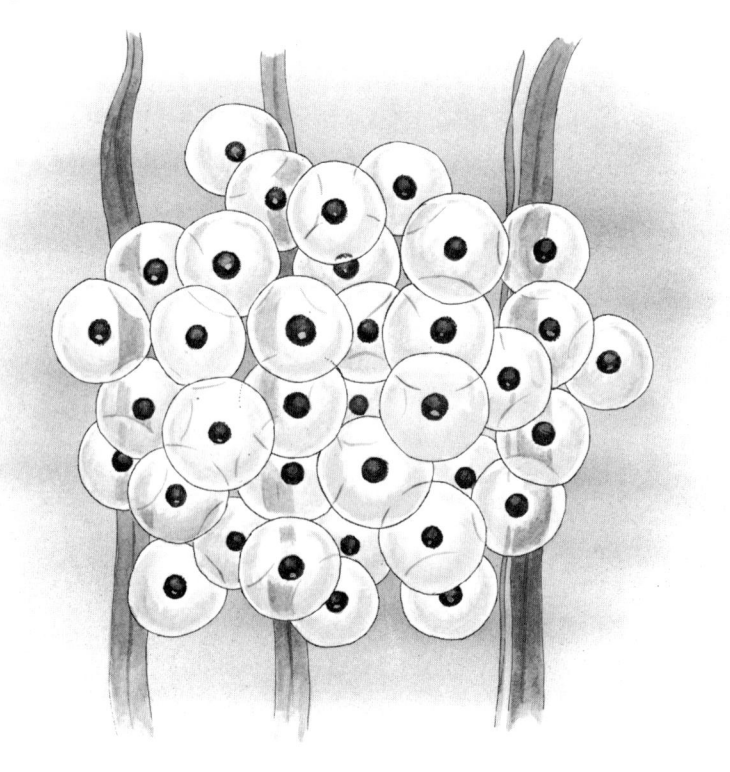

What do you think will happen to the eggs?

Do you remember how frogs' eggs turn into young frogs?
See if you can tell the story in your own words.
You can use these pictures to help you.

1

2
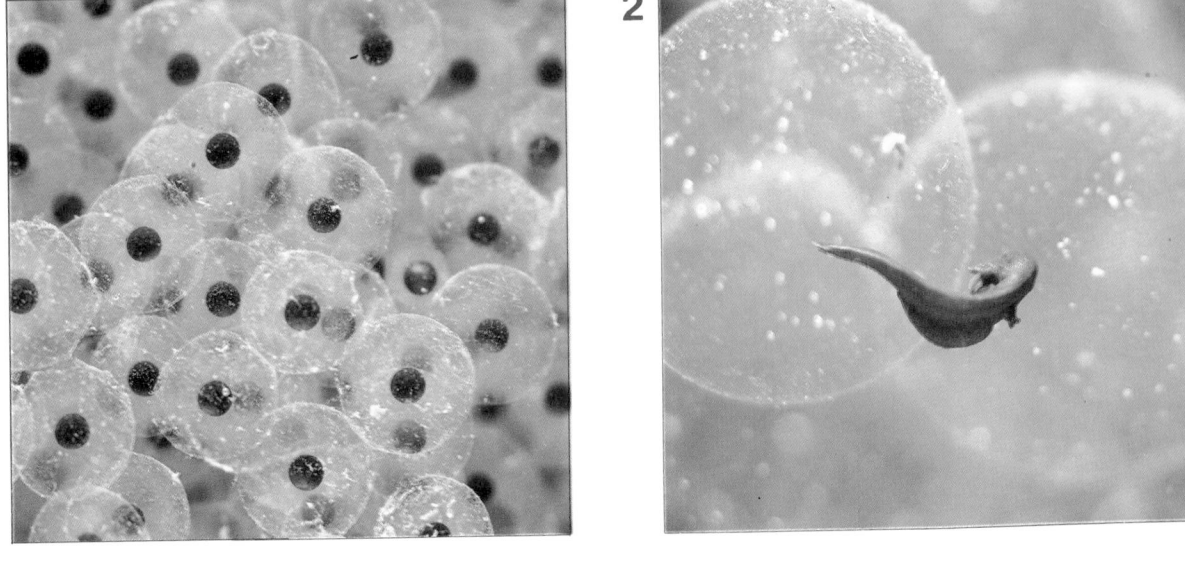

4

5

Index

This index will help you to find some of the important words in the book

3

6

you want to watch tadpoles grow, try keeping them in a bowl.
ut don't forget to put in a stone that sticks out of the water.